SPOTLIGHT ON GEORGIA

GEORGIA DURING THE ERA OF WESTWARD EXPANSION 1789 TO 1840

SAM CROMPTON

PowerKiDS press™

NEW YORK

Published in 2018 by The Rosen Publishing Group, Inc.
29 East 21st Street, New York, NY 10010

Editor: Theresa Morlock
Book Design: Rachel Rising

Photo Credits: Cover courtesy of the Georgia Historical Society; p. 4 Collegiate Images/Collegiate Images/ Getty Images; p. 5 Jim Pruitt/Shutterstock.com; p. 7 White, Rev. George. Histrorical Collection of Georgia. New York, NY: Pudney & Russell Publishers, 1855; pp. 7, 17 (background) Reinhold Leitner/Shutterstock.com; p. 8 https://commons.wikimedia.org/wiki/File:Yazoo-Georgia_Controversy.png; p. 9 Hulton Archive/Stringer/Getty Images; p. 11 National Archives and Records Administration/Records of the Patent and Trademark Office/Record Group 241; p. 13 https://commons.wikimedia.org/wiki/File:AtlantaNegroSalesLOC.jpg; p. 15 https://commons.wikimedia.org/wiki/File:Benjamin_Hawkins_and_the_Creek_Indians.jpg; p. 17 Proceedings of the Massachusetts Historical Society 1803; p. 19 Charles Phelps Cushing/ClassicStock/Getty Images; p. 21 Archive Photos/Stringer/Getty Images; p. 23 Rob Hainer/Shutterstock.com; p. 23 https://commons.wikimedia.org/wiki/File:Gold_Battle_Branch.jpg; p. 25 Historical/Contributor/Getty Images; p. 27 https://commons.wikimedia.org/wiki/File:Worcester.jpg; p. 28 courtesy of the Library of Congress; p. 29 https://commons.wikimedia.org/wiki/File:Trails_of_Tears_en.png.

Cataloging-in-Publication Data
Names: Crompton, Sam.
Title: Georgia during the era of westward expansion / Sam Crompton.
Description: New York : PowerKids Press, 2018. | Series: Spotlight on Georgia | Includes index.
Identifiers: ISBN 9781508160168 (pbk.) | ISBN 9781508160199 (library bound) | ISBN 9781508160175 (6 pack)
Subjects: LCSH: Georgia--History--1775-1865--Juvenile literature.
Classification: LCC F290.C76 2018 | DDC 975.8'03 --dc23

Manufactured in the United States of America

CPSIA Compliance Information: Batch #BS17PK For further information contact Rosen Publishing, New York, New York at 1-800-237-9932.

CONTENTS

CHAPTER ONE

POSTWAR GEORGIA

In the years following the American Revolution, Georgia underwent many changes. Its educational and political systems improved. On January 27, 1785, the Georgia General Assembly founded the University of Georgia, making Georgia the first state to take steps toward state-funded universities. The creation of the University of Georgia laid the foundation for the system of higher education throughout the United States.

In 1803, the United States and France made a land deal known as the Louisiana Purchase. This deal doubled the size of the United States.

On January 2, 1788, Georgia became the fourth state to **ratify** the U.S. Constitution. Georgia's own constitution, which had taken effect in 1777, was changed to reflect the new U.S. Constitution. As the new state began to take shape, westward **expansion** became the leading issue. In American history, westward expansion refers to the United States government gaining territories in the western part of the continent. The government achieved westward expansion by buying land, fighting wars, making treaties, and forcibly removing American Indians.

CHAPTER TWO

GEORGIA'S LAND POLICIES

In the years leading up to the 1800s, Georgia put land policies into practice that aimed to remove American Indians and expand white settlement westward. The headright system was the first of these policies. This system granted land to people who agreed to settle in certain areas. Headright laws were first created in 1618 when the British settled Jamestown, Virginia, as a way to draw settlers to work the land.

Georgia passed its first headright law in 1777. It didn't grant any land under such a law until 1783. Under a new headright law passed in 1780, the state offered families 200 acres (80.9 ha) of land plus 50 acres (20.2 ha) per person to move to Georgia. After the American Revolution, however, Georgia politicians began to grant much larger amounts of land than were legally allowed. This led to a series of problems in the state.

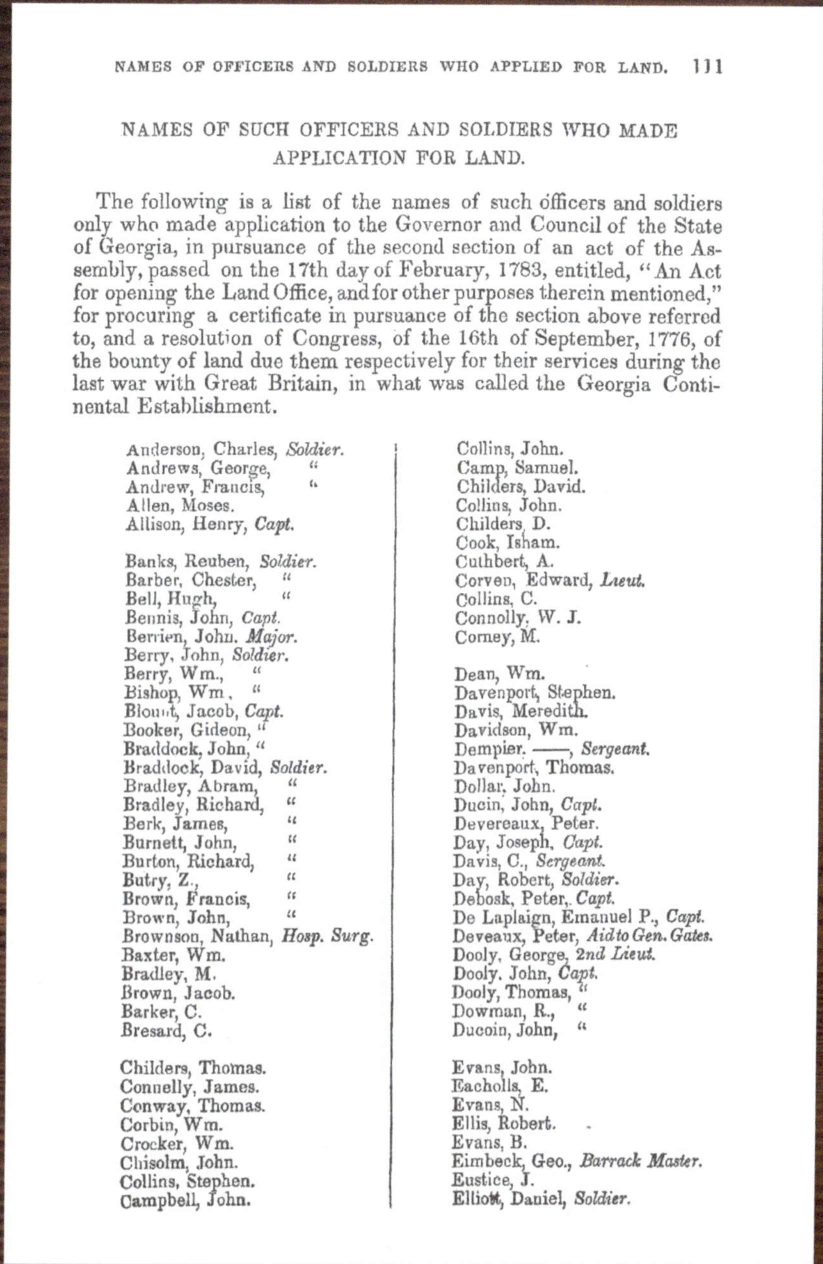

NAMES OF OFFICERS AND SOLDIERS WHO APPLIED FOR LAND. 111

NAMES OF SUCH OFFICERS AND SOLDIERS WHO MADE APPLICATION FOR LAND.

The following is a list of the names of such officers and soldiers only who made application to the Governor and Council of the State of Georgia, in pursuance of the second section of an act of the Assembly, passed on the 17th day of February, 1783, entitled, "An Act for opening the Land Office, and for other purposes therein mentioned," for procuring a certificate in pursuance of the section above referred to, and a resolution of Congress, of the 16th of September, 1776, of the bounty of land due them respectively for their services during the last war with Great Britain, in what was called the Georgia Continental Establishment.

Anderson, Charles, *Soldier.*
Andrews, George, "
Andrew, Francis, "
Allen, Moses.
Allison, Henry, *Capt.*

Banks, Reuben, *Soldier.*
Barber, Chester, "
Bell, Hugh, "
Bennis, John, *Capt.*
Berrien, John, *Major.*
Berry, John, *Soldier.*
Berry, Wm., "
Bishop, Wm., "
Blount, Jacob, *Capt.*
Booker, Gideon, "
Braddock, John, "
Braddock, David, *Soldier.*
Bradley, Abram, "
Bradley, Richard, "
Berk, James, "
Burnett, John, "
Burton, Richard, "
Butry, Z., "
Brown, Francis, "
Brown, John, "
Brownson, Nathan, *Hosp. Surg.*
Baxter, Wm.
Bradley, M.
Brown, Jacob.
Barker, C.
Bresard, C.

Childers, Thomas.
Connelly, James.
Conway, Thomas.
Corbin, Wm.
Crocker, Wm.
Chisolm, John.
Collins, Stephen.
Campbell, John.
Collins, John.
Camp, Samuel.
Childers, David.
Collins, John.
Childers, D.
Cook, Isham.
Cuthbert, A.
Corven, Edward, *Lieut.*
Collins, C.
Connolly, W. J.
Corney, M.

Dean, Wm.
Davenport, Stephen.
Davis, Meredith.
Davidson, Wm.
Dempier, ——, *Sergeant.*
Davenport, Thomas.
Dollar, John.
Ducin, John, *Capt.*
Devereaux, Peter.
Day, Joseph, *Capt.*
Davis, C., *Sergeant.*
Day, Robert, *Soldier.*
Debosk, Peter, *Capt.*
De Laplaign, Emanuel P., *Capt.*
Deveaux, Peter, *Aid to Gen. Gates.*
Dooly, George, *2nd Lieut.*
Dooly, John, *Capt.*
Dooly, Thomas, "
Dowman, R., "
Ducoin, John, "

Evans, John.
Eacholls, E.
Evans, N.
Ellis, Robert.
Evans, B.
Eimbeck, Geo., *Barrack Master.*
Eustice, J.
Elliott, Daniel, *Soldier.*

After the war, many veterans applied for land grants meant to reward them for their service to the country. This document shows the names of the officers applying for land in Georgia in 1783.

CHAPTER THREE

THE YAZOO LAND FRAUD

Georgia's western territories, which now make up much of Mississippi and Alabama, were referred to as the Yazoo lands because of the Yazoo River that runs through them. In 1795, Georgia legislators sold 35 million acres (14.2 million ha) of the Yazoo lands to four companies for $500,000. This was much less than the land was worth. In return, many officials received money and land for their support of the sale.

This map shows the areas of land involved in the Yazoo land **fraud**.

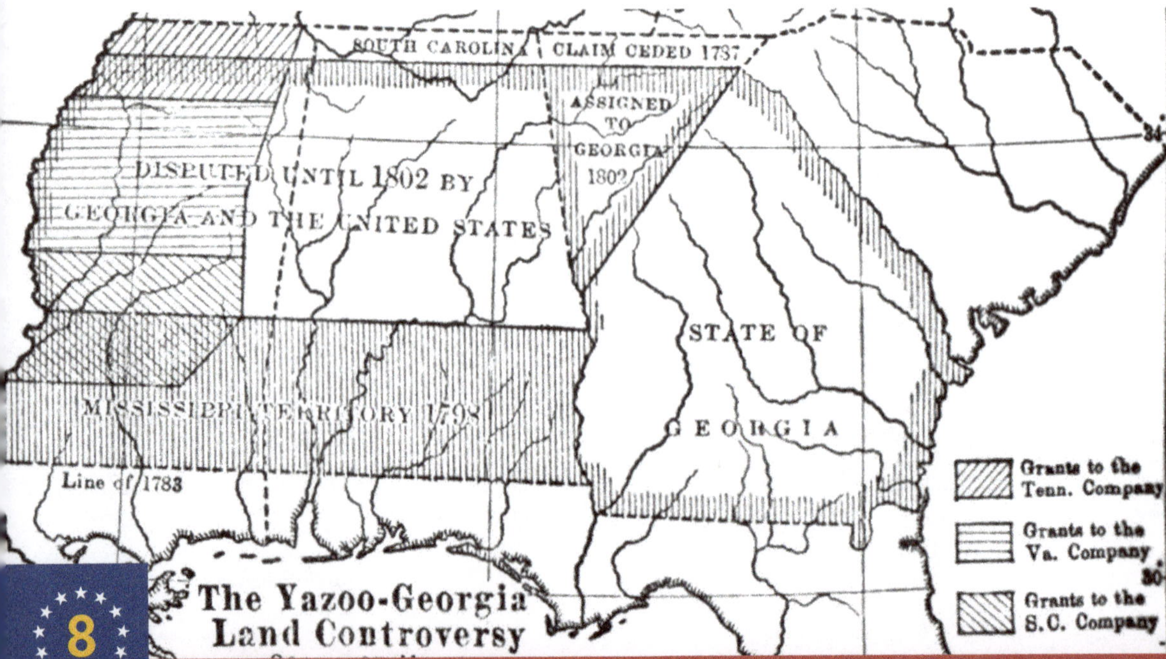

James Jackson was a senator from Georgia. He helped overturn the Yazoo sale and replace the guilty legislators.

This angered the people of Georgia, many of whom felt that the state legislators had acted in their own interests and not the people's. In 1796, the people elected new legislators, who canceled the sale and returned the money. The companies that had bought the land and the people to whom they had sold some of it continued to fight to reclaim it. In 1802, Georgia granted the Yazoo lands to the U.S. government.

CHAPTER FOUR

THE COTTON KINGDOM

Georgia's growth was aided by the many **technological** advancements in the late 18th and early 19th centuries. Railroads began to expand, further opening the West to trade and development. In 1794, Eli Whitney **patented** the cotton gin, which was a machine designed to remove the seeds from cotton. This invention meant that cotton could be processed much faster than it could before. This was especially important in Georgia, where cotton was a major crop and the economy depended on it.

Following the invention of the cotton gin, cotton production in Georgia spiked. Although this helped the Georgia economy, it also contributed to the expansion of slavery. Slaves were used to grow and pick the cotton, which could be sold and shipped at increasingly high rates as other technological advancements were made. Of all the southern states, Georgia had the most slaves.

Shown above is the original patent drawing for the cotton gin. The cotton gin allowed two people to do the work that had once been done by 50.

CHAPTER FIVE

SLAVERY IN GEORGIA

By 1800, there were about 59,700 slaves in Georgia. Before the African slave trade was banned in 1808, some 48,000 Africans were shipped into Georgia. Although the end of the slave trade cut off the shipment of slaves into the country, slave trading continued within the United States. The population of slaves continued to rise as slaves had babies.

Most Georgia slaves worked on rice or cotton plantations, doing hard physical labor from dawn to dusk. They often lived in unhealthy conditions and suffered mistreatment from their white masters. Thousands of families were torn apart by the slave trade within the country as parents and children and husbands and wives were sold and transported against their will. Slaveholders made up less than half of the population, but the wealth and power they held allowed them to **dominate** Georgia society.

This image shows a slave market in Atlanta, Georgia, in 1864.

CHAPTER SIX

RACIAL DIVISIONS

At the turn of the century, nearly everyone in Georgia depended on farming but the people were racially divided. The three main groups were white settlers, black slaves, and American Indians.

During the 1790s, the U.S. government adopted a "plan of civilization" to deal with American Indians who they viewed as an **obstacle** to westward expansion. The plan involved settling the Indians on small farms so they would be willing to peacefully give up their hunting territories. During the early 1800s, the Creek, Cherokee, Choctaw, Chickasaw, and Seminole Indians became known as the "Five Civilized Tribes" because they adopted parts of the white setters' ways and culture.

In some ways, voluntary **assimilation** was helpful to American Indians. However, it often meant giving up cultural beliefs and traditions. Many people resisted forced assimilation and refused to change to live according to white rules.

Using the word "civilized" to set more assimilated nations apart from others shows that white Americans thought of American Indians that continued their traditional lifestyles as "uncivilized" or "savage."

CHAPTER SEVEN

THE PLAN OF CIVILIZATION

Born in North Carolina, Benjamin Hawkins came to Georgia in 1796 to act as the U.S. agent for relations with the area's American Indians. Over the next 20 years, Hawkins persuaded many American Indians—among them Creeks, Cherokees, and Choctaws—to live more like white people. Some American Indians built sawmills to cut logs for building and gristmills to grind grain into flour. Others grew cotton and potatoes. Some even owned black slaves.

Hawkins may have believed that farming could help American Indians survive without relying on hunting as their lands were taken by the government and white settlers. If they lived in towns and participated in white society, some might be treated with less violence and hatred by white settlers. In another sense, assimilation represented a death of tribal culture. However, even assimilated American Indians continued to face **prejudice** from white people.

The Indians in the south western parts of the United States proper, or in the states of Tennessee, Georgia and Missisippi territory, are the following:

Tribes.	Warriors.	Souls.	Gratuities.	Perpetual Annuities. merchan.	cash.
Cherokees	3000	12395	$23200	$600	$3000
Chickesaws	1000	3500	29000		3000
Chactaws	4000	15000	54000		3000
Creeks	5000	20000	231000		4800
Total,	13000	50895	$337200	$600	$13800
Total of the Tribes between the Ohio and the Lakes.	5204	19220	79487	9500	9250
Total in the U. S. west of the Alleghany mountains.	18204	70115	416687	10100	23050

Of the tribes in the United States proper, the Cherokees, Chickesaws and Chactaws appear the most favourable for the establishment of a mission with the prospect of success. To the Cherokees, the general assembly of the Presbyterian Church have turned their attention, and are looking for missionaries of a proper character, to send among them. This tribe, therefore, we will leave out of consideration, and take a view of the others—Chickesaws and Chactaws. These two tribes are more numerous than the aggregate of all the tribes between the Ohio and the lakes; and also speak the same language. From these circumstances solely, other things being equal, a mission would be more desirable, and the prospect of success greater, than among either of, the small tribes in Indiana or Illinoi. There are other reasons which induce us to give these nations the preference. They have already made great progress in agriculture and civilization, and are by degrees casting off the Indian habit, and adopting the modes of the whites. They are generally removin out of their villages, giving up the hunting life, clearin small plantations, and raising domestick animals. Th have already experienced, many of them, the blessir which flow from this change of habits, and are anxiou make further improvements; and many of them feel

The report above is a record of the major tribes in the Georgia region in 1803. The document notes which tribes seemed to be assimilating the most.

CHAPTER EIGHT

THE CREEK WAR

Also called the Red Stick War, the Creek War of 1813 to 1814 was fought between the United States, different **factions** of the Creek Nation, and Britain. It took place during the War of 1812, a conflict between Britain and the United States that lasted from 1812 to 1815. The Creek War began as a civil war between the Creeks and a Creek faction called the Red Sticks. The Red Sticks fought to resist assimilation and white expansion into Creek territories. As a result of the Treaty of Fort Wilkinson, which was signed in 1802, Georgia had gained more Creek land. The state capital was moved west from Louisville to Milledgeville.

Americans fought against the Red Sticks with the help of Choctaw and Cherokee warriors. The British sided with the Red Stick Creeks. The war ended with American victory, resulting in further white expansion.

The Battle of Horseshoe Bend ended the Creek War. This illustration shows General Andrew Jackson meeting with Red Eagle Weatherford after the Red Sticks were defeated.

CHAPTER NINE

WILLIAM MCINTOSH

William McIntosh was a chief of the Creek Nation who supported assimilation and helped the U.S. government claim Creek territories in Georgia. During the Creek War, McIntosh fought alongside the U.S. troops under the command of General Andrew Jackson at the Battle of Horseshoe Bend. Jackson's victory led to the Treaty of Fort Jackson, under which the Creeks lost 22 million acres (8.9 million ha) of land in Alabama and Georgia.

Many Creeks felt **betrayed** by McIntosh's support for the United States. The treaty resulted in lost land, starvation, and more suffering for their people. In 1821, the Treaty of Indian Springs took more Creek land in exchange for food and supplies. McIntosh received over 1,000 acres (404.7 ha) of land for his help **negotiating** this treaty. In 1825, he and five other Creek chiefs signed the Second Treaty of Indian Springs, which sold almost all Creek lands in Georgia to the U.S. government for a very low price. McIntosh was executed by Creek chief Menawa the same year.

McIntosh's father was a white man from Scotland, and his mother was a Creek woman. He was also known as *Tustunnuggee Hutkee*, which means "White Warrior" in the Creek language.

CHAPTER TEN

THE DAHLONEGA GOLD RUSH

From 1805 to 1832, the Georgia legislature created policies that forcibly removed American Indians from their territories and granted the land to white settlers through a **lottery** system.

In 1828 or 1829, gold was discovered in northern Georgia in what was then the land of the Cherokee people. Thousands of miners came into Cherokee lands and set up mining towns, the largest of which was Dahlonega, Georgia. The Cherokee people objected to miners taking over their lands, but they received no help from the government, which benefited from the discovery of gold in the region.

Andrew Jackson became the U.S. president in March 1829. He was quick to try to remove Indians from the southeastern states. He had fought the Creek Indians at the Battle of Horseshoe Bend and was strongly prejudiced against them. Jackson's influence led Congress to pass the Indian Removal Act of 1830.

Traces of gold can be seen in this piece of rock, which was mined in Lumpkin County, Georgia.

CHAPTER ELEVEN

THE INDIAN REMOVAL ACT

The Indian Removal Act granted the president power to negotiate removal treaties with American Indians living east of the Mississippi River. Removed nations would be granted territories west of the Mississippi. This territory had not yet been taken over by white settlers. Those nations that chose to stay east of the Mississippi would be granted citizenship within their states. The Indian Removal Act appeared to offer a peaceful option to American Indians. In reality, however, most removal was forced and often resulted in violence.

The Indian Removal Act led to the forced removal of many southeastern peoples, including the Choctaws, Creeks, Seminoles, and Cherokees. During Jackson's presidency, the government removed 46,000 American Indians from their territories. Over 25 million acres (10 million ha) of land that once belonged to American Indians was opened to white settlers, who used much of it to grow cotton.

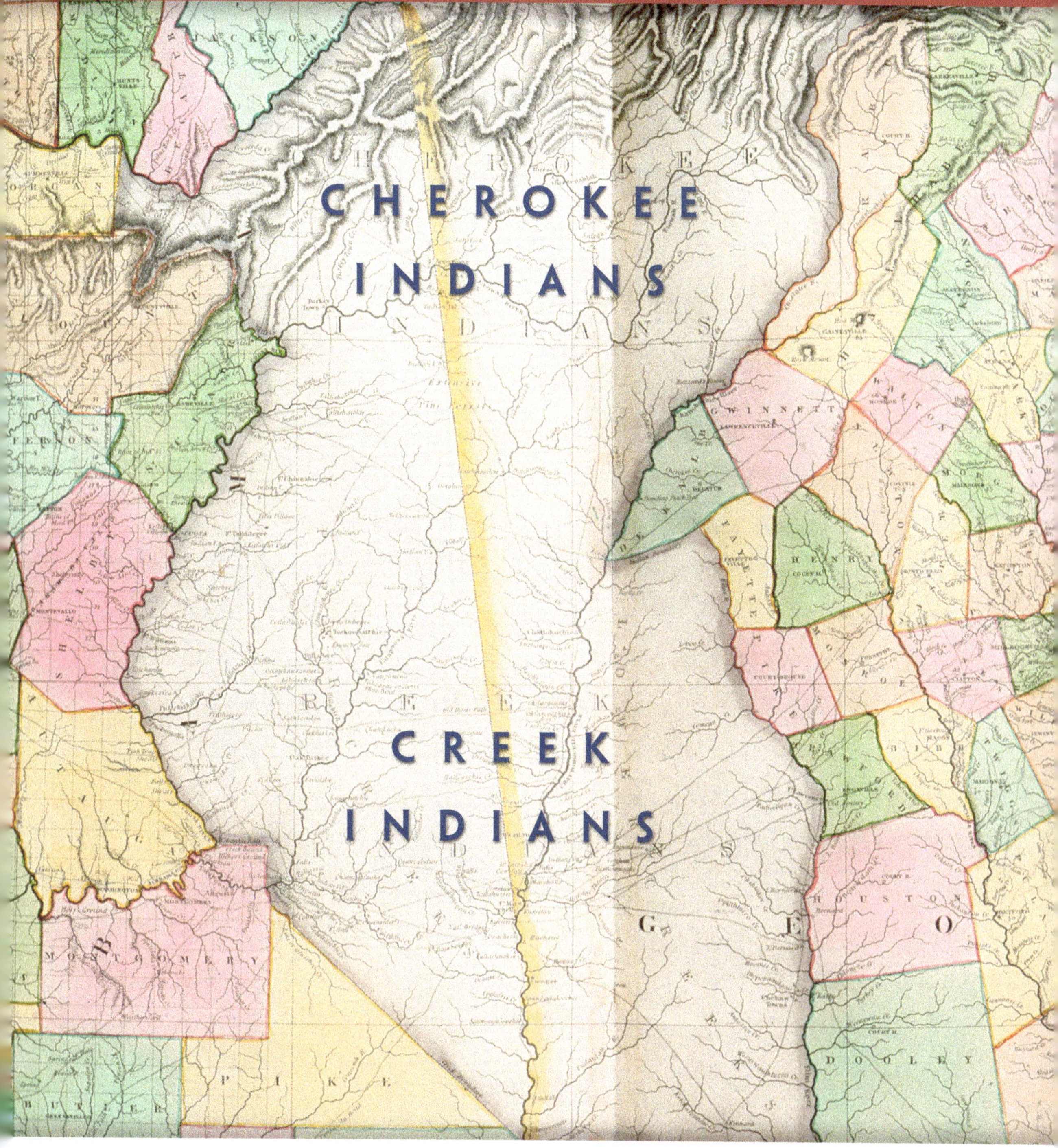

This map shows the land belonging to the Cherokee and Creek people before the Indian Removal Act.

CHAPTER TWELVE

WORCESTER V. GEORGIA

In 1832, the U.S. Supreme Court ruled on an important case about how state governments dealt with American Indians. The case concerned a white minister named Samuel Worcester who lived with the Cherokee people on their land within Georgia. Worcester was arrested because it was illegal for a white person to live on Cherokee land. Worcester argued that Georgia's laws couldn't be enforced in the Cherokee territory because it was a sovereign, or independent nation.

The Supreme Court, under Chief Justice John Marshall, ruled in Worcester's favor. This meant American Indian nations would be treated as sovereign nations that were independent from state laws. President Jackson ignored the court's ruling, demanding that the Cherokee Nation be moved west. Although the government failed to protect the rights of Cherokee Indians at the time, the Supreme Court's ruling would set the standard for the sovereignty of American Indian nations in the future.

Samuel Worcester was a Christian minister who worked closely with the Cherokees.

CHAPTER THIRTEEN

THE TRAIL OF TEARS

John Ross, a Cherokee chief, spoke out against attempts to steal his people's land. A few Cherokee people had signed an agreement called the Treaty of New Echota, in which they agreed to give up Cherokee lands. The treaty was not signed by the true Cherokee leaders and was therefore not lawful. Ross sent a **petition** with almost 16,000 signatures to the U.S. Senate to ask it to cancel the treaty, but the Senate ignored the petition.

When many of the Cherokees refused to leave their homes, the U.S. government sent troops to force them to march west. As the Cherokee were driven from their land, soldiers and white settlers stole their belongings and destroyed their homes.

JOHN ROSS

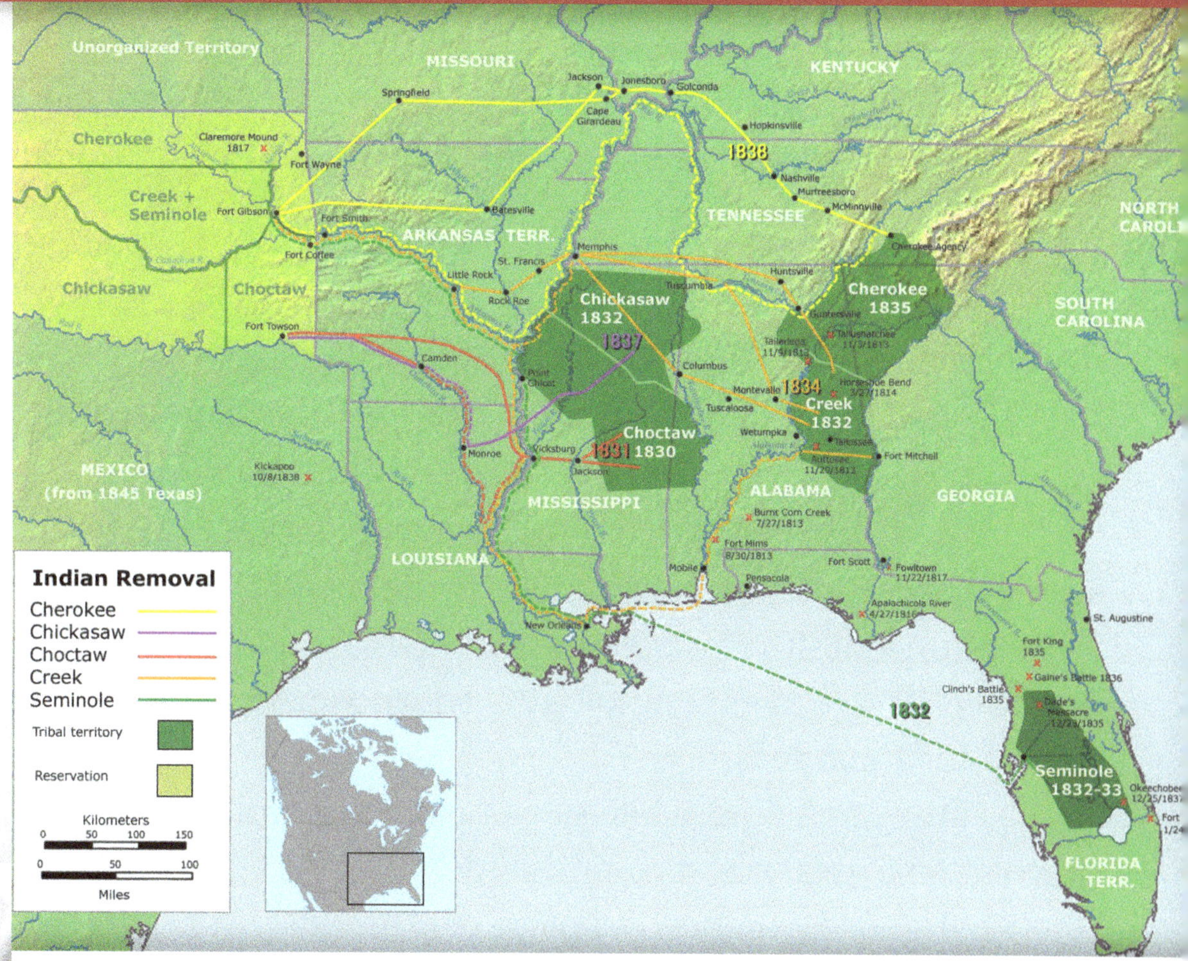

This map shows some of the paths taken when American Indians were forced off their lands during the 1830s.

About 15,000 Cherokees were forced to walk over 1,200 miles (1,931 km), and many died of starvation and disease along the way. This forced march, and similar experiences for other American Indians, came to be called the Trail of Tears. At least 4,000 Cherokee people lost their lives on this march.

CHAPTER FOURTEEN

A NEW GEORGIA

The period between 1789 and 1840 was marked by westward expansion, the forced relocation of American Indians, and the growth of slavery in Georgia. Both the state and federal governments waged war on American Indian nations and did their best to drive them west so white settlers could use their land to mine for gold and farm cotton. The cotton industry was built on the backs of slaves, whose numbers increased as technological advancements caused the cotton trade to boom.

At the same time, white slave-holding Georgians, Revolutionary War veterans, and settlers who received large grants of land experienced a period of prosperity. As the American Indians suffered **brutality** and forced removal and slaves endured violence and hard labor, white settlers profited. These racial divisions would continue to shape the state of Georgia for years to come.

GLOSSARY

assimilate (uh-SIH-muh-layt) To absorb, or blend into, the customs of a group of people.

betray (bih-TRAY) To turn against.

brutality (broo-TA-luh-tee) A harsh, unfeeling action against another.

dominate (DAH-muh-nayt) To rule over or to stand out above all others.

expansion (ihk-SPAN-shun) The act or process of making something bigger.

faction (FAK-shun) A group within a larger group.

fraud (FRAWD) An instance of using lies or tricks to cheat or to take advantage of a situation in a way that is against the law.

lottery (LAH-tuh-ree) The drawing of lots used to decide something. Lots are objects used as counters in a lottery.

negotiate (nih-GOH-shee-ayt) To discuss something formally in order to reach an agreement.

obstacle (AHB-stih-kuhl) Something that makes it difficult to complete an action.

patent (PA-tent) To be granted rights from the government to make, use, or sell an invention.

petition (puh-TIH-shun) A formal written request to a leader or government regarding a particular cause.

prejudice (PREH-juh-dis) An unfair feeling of dislike for a person or group because of race or religious or political beliefs.

ratify (RA-tih-fy) To approve or to agree to something in an official way.

technological (tehk-nuh-LAH-jih-kuhl) Of, related to, or using technology, which is a method that uses science to solve problems and the tools used to solve those problems.

INDEX

PRIMARY SOURCE LIST

Page 7
Names of officers and soldiers who applied for land. White, Rev. George. Historical Collections of Georgia. New York, NY: Pudney & Russell Publishers, 1855.

Page 11
Original patent drawing of the cotton gin. National Archives and Records Administration/Records of the Patent and Trademark Office/Record Group 241, 1793.

Page 17
Report on Cherokees. Proceedings of the Massachusetts Historical Society, 1803.

WEBSITES

Due to the changing nature of Internet links, PowerKids Press has developed an online list of websites related to the subject of this book. This site is updated regularly. Please use this link to access the list: www.powerkidslinks.com/sog/1789